Start Reading
AND LISTENING

Wait for Me!

First published in the UK in 2005 by
QED Publishing
A Quarto Group company
226 City Road
London EC1V 2TT
www.qed-publishing.co.uk

A Catalogue record for this book is available from the British Library.

ISBN 1 84538 442 3

Written and illustrated by Eileen Browne
Designed by Melissa Alaverdy
Editor Hannah Ray

Series Consultant Anne Faundez
Publisher Steve Evans
Creative Director Louise Morley
Editorial Manager Jean Coppendale

Printed and bound in China

Start Reading
AND LISTENING

Wait for Me!

Eileen Browne

QED Publishing

"I'm thirsty and hot,"
said Eddie the elephant.

"Me too," said Poppy
the parrot.

"So am I," said
Slippy the snake.

4

"I've got an idea!" said Molly the monkey.
"Let's go to the cool, sparkly river."

"Hooray!" said everybody.

"But how do we get to the cool, sparkly river?"
asked Eddie the elephant.

"It's easy!" said Poppy and Slippy and Molly.
"We cross the wide, sandy desert,
get past the huge pile of rocks,
push through the dark, tangled jungle
and go over the green, slimy swamp.
That's how we get to the cool, sparkly river.

Come on, follow us!"

They went to the wide, sandy desert.

"How can we cross it?"
asked Eddie the elephant.

"With a flap of my wings!" said Poppy.

"With a slither and a zig-zag,"
said Slippy.

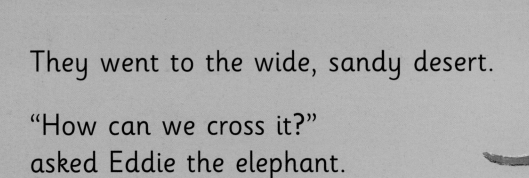

"With a hop and
a skip," said Molly.

"Let's go!"

Stomp, stomp, stompety-stomp went Eddie the elephant.

"Wait for me!"

They reached the huge pile of rocks.

"How can we get past them?" asked Eddie.

"With a flap and a hop," said Poppy.

"With a wiggle and a squeeze," said Slippy.

"With a scramble and a climb," said Molly.

Puff-pant, puff-pant, went Eddie.

"Wait for me!"

They came to the dark, tangly jungle.

"How can we get through it?" asked Eddie.

"With a flutter and a flap," said Poppy.

"With a weave and a waggle," said Slippy.

12

"With a swing and a leap," said Molly.

Crash, smash, bumpity-bash, went Eddie.

"Wait for me!"

13

They got to the green, slimy swamp.

"How can we go over it?" asked Eddie.

"With a flap and a glide," said Poppy.

"With a slither and a wriggle," said Slippy.

"With a run and a slide," said Molly.

Squish, squelch, splatter and splodge,
went Eddie.

"Wait for me!"

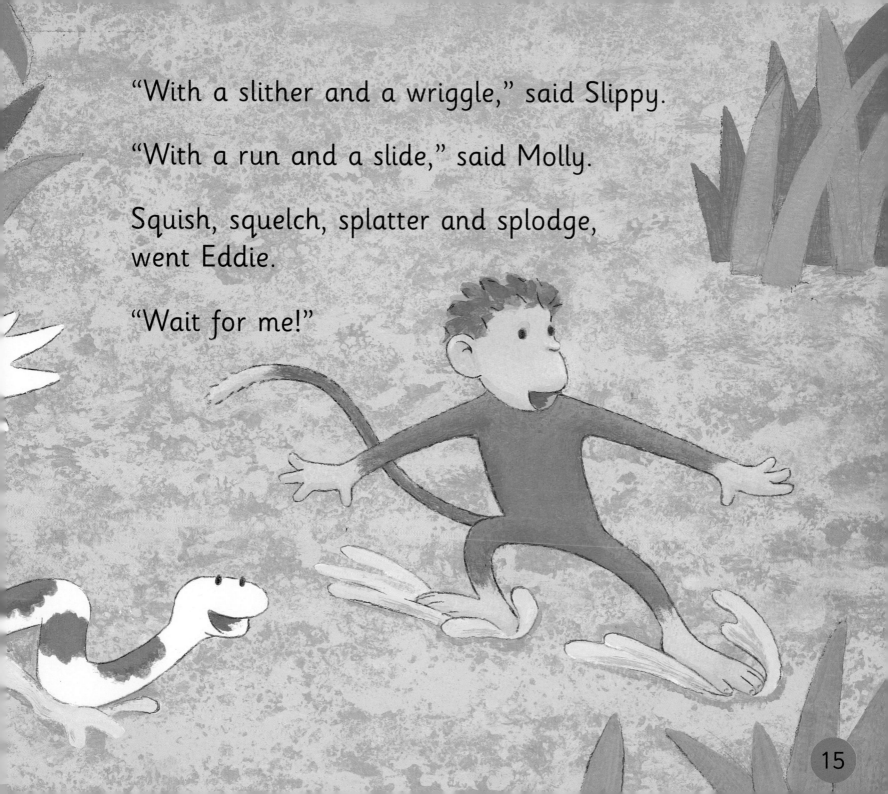

At last, they arrived at the cool, sparkly river.

"Shall we fly in?" said Poppy the parrot.

"Shall we slip in?" said Slippy the snake.

"Shall we climb in?" said Molly the monkey.

"Go in how you like ... I'm JUMPING," said Eddie.

And Poppy and Slippy and Molly all shouted,

"Hey! Wait for me!"

What do you think?

Can you remember the
names of the animals?

Which is your
favourite character?

Can you go stomp, stomp, stompety-stomp just like Eddie the elephant?

Can you flap and hop like Poppy the parrot?

Can you slither and wriggle like Slippy the snake?

Can you name one of the landscapes that the animals need to cross before they get to the cool, sparkly river?

How does Molly get across the green, slimy swamp?

How does Eddie get into the river?

Parents' and teachers' notes

- Look at the cover together and predict what the story may be about.
- Introduce the term 'character' and explain that Slippy the snake, Molly the monkey, Poppy the parrot and Eddie the elephant are all characters.
- Can your child paint a picture of his or her favourite character?
- Together, look at the pictures and talk with your child about what is happening on each page.
- Read aloud the characters' names – Slippy the snake, Molly the monkey, Poppy the parrot and Eddie the elephant. As you do so, emphasize the initial letter sounds, 's', 'm', 'p' and 'e'. Can your child distinguish these sounds?
- Together think up some alliterative names for alternative characters, for example, Hatty the hen, Slimy the snail.
- Find some more alliterative words in the text, for example, 'weave and waggle', 'splatter and splodge,' 'flutter and flap'.

- Can your child remember the words the animals use to describe how they should enter the cool, sparkly river (i.e., 'fly', 'slip', 'climb' and 'jump in')? Can he or she think of any other movement words?
- Explain that dialogue is contained within speech marks (inverted commas) and that each character's speech is set out on a new line.
- Read the story aloud, using a different voice for each character. Choose some lines from the story and have fun practising reading with expression.
- With a group of four children acting out the characters, and you acting as the narrator, perform the story and set it to music. What sort of music and movements would suit each animal? For example, Eddie the elephant might move to loud drumming music and move with large and lumbering gestures; Slippy the snake might move to the soft shaking of maracas and move with small, sinuous gestures. Experiment with a variety of different sound effects and movements.